'The Church of England is ca[lled] [to share the good] news of God's salvation thro[ugh] [Jesus Christ. The life] of our communities and insti[tutions is integral to] how we address this task. The [good news] speaks of welcome for all, with a particular regard for those who are most vulnerable, into a community where the value and dignity of every human being is affirmed and those in positions of responsibility and authority are truly trustworthy. Being faithful to our call to share the gospel therefore compels us to take with the utmost seriousness the challenge of preventing abuse from happening and responding well where it has.'

From 'Promoting a Safer Church', The Church of England's Safeguarding Policy Statement

Message from the Most Revd and Rt Honourable Justin Welby, Archbishop of Canterbury

Dear Colleagues

Safeguarding is at the heart of our Christian faith. We are all made unique and in the image of God. Jesus came that we might have life and have it in abundance (see John 10.10).

'Safeguarding' means the action the Church takes to promote a safer culture in all our churches. In order to achieve this we need to do a lot of hard work. We will promote the welfare of children, young people and adults. We will work to prevent abuse from occurring. We will seek to protect those who are at risk of being abused and respond well to those who have been abused. We will take care to identify where a person may present a risk to others, and offer support to them whilst taking steps to mitigate such risks.

The Church will take appropriate steps to maintain a safer environment for all. In order to do this we must be obedient to Christ who placed a child in the midst of his disciples and encourages us all to be childlike in our faith (see Matthew 18.1-5). So we must practise fully and positively a ministry to all children, young people and adults, and respond sensitively and compassionately to their needs in order to help keep them safe from harm.

This Parish Handbook aims to further strengthen the Church's approach to safeguarding by bringing into one place the safeguarding responsibilities for parishes as outlined in the House of Bishops' Safeguarding Policy and Practice Guidance. It has been designed to support the day-to-day work of all parishes in relation to safeguarding and those who have a key role to play with children, young people and adults who may be vulnerable.

It is complemented by a pocket safeguarding guide, a contact safeguarding card and a Parish Safeguarding Resource Pack that offers a range of model templates and good practice reference material.

It has been informed by best practice in faith organisations and the safeguarding sector. I want to thank very much all those who were involved in the work and all those who contributed to the consultation process and offered their helpful and informed views.

The House of Bishops commends this practice guidance for use by all parishes, particularly the safeguarding lead on the Parochial Church Council, clergy, Parish Safeguarding Officers, licensed lay ministers and leaders of parishes who work with children, young people and vulnerable adults.

I hope that this Handbook and complementary guides and templates will contribute greatly to promoting a safer culture and building good safeguarding practice in your parish church.

I hold in my prayers all who are directly involved in this crucial work and let us all pray that we may strive to be a safe church for all.

Yours in Christ's fellowship,

Archbishop Justin Welby

Church House Publishing
Church House
Great Smith Street
London SW1P 3AZ
www.chpublishing.co.uk

Parish Safeguarding Handbook
ISBN 978 0 7151 1138 3

Published 2018 for the House of Bishops
of the Church of England by Church House Publishing

Design and typesetting by Fordesign

Printed in the UK by Core Publications

Contents

Introduction

- The handbook brings into one place the key safeguarding responsibilities for parishes that are outlined in the House of Bishops' Safeguarding Policy and Practice Guidance. It is not exhaustive but is designed to support the day-to-day safeguarding work of parishes. The handbook signposts to more detailed guidance that can be accessed as required.

- The handbook is aimed at all those who have a key role to play with children, young people[1] and adults in a parish. This is envisaged to be predominantly the incumbent and the Parish Safeguarding Officer but will be dependent on the size of the parish and the number of other roles it may have. Section 1 is specifically aimed at the incumbent and those that chair and/or are the safeguarding lead[2] on the Parochial Church Council. Sections 10, 11 and 12 are specifically aimed at leaders of the parish's work with children, young people and adults.

- The handbook is complemented by an A3 policy poster, a pocket safeguarding guide, a safeguarding contact card and a range of online parish safeguarding resources that offer model templates and good practice reference material. It is recommended that the pocket guide is made available to all those in the parish who have a role with children, young people and adults, including volunteers. The safeguarding contact card is an additional quick guide that is also available to all involved in the parish. It is ultimately up to local determination how to use the pocket guide and contact card.

- For parish churches that share a Parish Safeguarding Officer, the handbook may also be used as a joint Parish Safeguarding Handbook.

- It is hoped that the use of the handbook and complementary material will contribute greatly to promoting a safer culture and building good safeguarding practice in a parish church.

- Please see the House of Bishops' Glossary for information on the language and terminology used in the handbook.

- Please see the appendix for more information on the term 'vulnerable adult'.

- The duty to have 'due regard' to guidance under section 5 of the Safeguarding and Clergy Discipline Measure 2016[3] applies to the handbook. It does not apply to the model templates and additional good practice reference material that have been offered to complement this handbook.

- In addition, failure to have due regard to House of Bishops' Safeguarding Policy and Practice Guidance may have direct consequences for the validity of your insurance.

- The most up-to-date version of the handbook will always be available on the Church of England website at **www.churchofengland.org/safeguarding**

Key messages

- The welfare of the child, young person and vulnerable adult is at all times paramount, and takes precedence over all other considerations.

- The Diocesan Safeguarding Adviser (DSA) must be consulted whenever a safeguarding concern of any kind arises in your parish.

- Safeguarding is part of our core faith and an integral feature of Christian life in our parish churches.

This symbol appears next to resources and templates that are available online at www.churchofengland.org/safeguarding

Quick Guide to the Handbook

1. Parish Roles and Responsibilities[4]

Parochial Church Council (PCC) and the incumbent

The PCC is the main decision maker of a parish. Its members are clergy, church wardens[5] and others elected by the Annual Parochial Church Meeting (APCM) of the parish. The PCC and the incumbent have a duty of care to ensure the protection of the vulnerable in their church community. In terms of safeguarding, the incumbent and the PCC will:

Adopt and implement

- The House of Bishops' Safeguarding Policy 'Promoting a Safer Church' (see A3 poster or the Model Parish Safeguarding Policy[6] ❶).

Appoint

- An appropriately experienced[7], named Parish Safeguarding Officer to work with the incumbent and the Parochial Church Council or join with other parishes to share a named Parish Safeguarding Officer[8] (see Model Parish Safeguarding Officer Role Description ❶).

Safer recruitment, support and training

- Have a policy statement on the recruitment of ex-offenders and ensure all those responsible for working with children, young people and vulnerable adults on behalf of the church are safely recruited (see section 5).

- Ensure all church officers are aware of the safeguarding policy/guidance and are trained appropriately for their roles (see section 6).

- Provide appropriate insurance to cover for all activities undertaken in the name of the Parochial Church Council which involve children, young people and adults.

Display

- A formal statement of adoption of the House of Bishops' 'Promoting a Safer Church: Safeguarding Policy Statement'. This should be signed on behalf of the PCC.

- Ensure information is displayed about how to contact the DSA(s), Parish Safeguarding Officer and how to get help outside the church with child and adult safeguarding issues (see Model Safeguarding in Your Parish – Who's Who ⊕).

- Ensure that safeguarding arrangements are clearly visible on the front page of the parish website[9].

Respond

- Have a procedure in place to deal promptly with safeguarding allegations or suspicions of abuse (see section 7).

- Report all safeguarding concerns or allegations including those against church officers to the Parish Safeguarding Officer/ incumbent and the DSA (see section 7).

- Ensure that known offenders or others who may pose a risk to children and/or vulnerable adults are effectively managed and monitored in consultation with the DSA (see section 10).

- Comply with all data protection legislation especially in regard to using (e.g. storing) information about any church officers and any safeguarding records.

- Ensure an 'activity risk assessment' is completed and reviewed regularly for each activity which is associated with either children or vulnerable adults and run in the name of the church (see Model Activity Risk Assessment Template ❶).

Review and report progress

- The PSO should regularly report on safeguarding in the parish. Safeguarding should be a standing agenda item at each PCC meeting[10]. At the APCM the PCC should provide an annual report in relation to safeguarding. In the PCC's annual report will be a statement which reports on progress and a statement as to whether or not the PCC has complied with the duty to have 'due regard' to the House of Bishops' Safeguarding Policy and Practice Guidance.[11]

Hire out church premises

- Ensure an addendum to a hire agreement is always used when any person/body hires church premises (i.e. a church building or a church hall) for activity that involves children, young people or vulnerable adults[12], for example a pre-school, youth group or mental health support group (see Model Safeguarding Provision for Church Premises Hire ❶).

Working in an LEP

- If working within Local Ecumenical Partnerships (LEPs), agree which denomination or organisation's safeguarding policy to follow, including where to seek advice in urgent situations in line with the practice guidance. This decision should be ratified both by the bishop and other appropriate church leaders in the partnership and shared with the DSA; in the event of a specific safeguarding concern, ensure that all the LEP partners are notified.

During a clergy vacancy[13]

- The PCC must, working with the church wardens, ensure that all information about safeguarding matters is securely stored before passing the information on to the new incumbent. The departing incumbent must give the safeguarding information to the Parish Safeguarding Officer who can pass the information on to the new incumbent when he/she takes up his/her new role.

Assurance check

Assess your parish's safeguarding arrangements, identify strengths and areas that need further work by using the Parish Safeguarding Checklist ❶. In addition, the diocese may also have its own parish safeguarding audit format.

2. What can a Parish Expect from the Diocese?

Safeguarding policy and guidance

The diocese is responsible for supporting parishes in implementing the House of Bishops' Safeguarding Policy and Practice Guidance. This includes arrangements to monitor the quality of safeguarding arrangements in parishes.

Safeguarding advice and support

The diocese has DSA(s) who are experienced safeguarding professionals who offer safeguarding advice and support to parishes. The parish **must** report any safeguarding concerns or allegations to the DSA within 24 hours of a concern arising. DSAs will advise on how to respond well. They will manage all concerns or allegations against church officers. The diocese offers an out-of-hours service for any safeguarding concerns or allegations that arise outside normal office hours.

Safeguarding training

The diocese is responsible for the provision of safeguarding training.

Safer recruitment support

The diocese is available for advice on all aspects of safer recruitment, including applications for a DBS check, mostly via a commissioned DBS provider. The DSA is also the person who risk assesses any blemished Disclosure and Barring Service (DBS) checks.

External scrutiny of safeguarding

The diocese has a group of senior clergy, church officers and external safeguarding professionals, independently chaired by an external safeguarding expert. The group is responsible for overseeing the implementation of policy, training and the effectiveness and quality of safeguarding arrangements. Details of the group can be found on the diocesan website[14].

Complaints procedure

The diocese has a complaints procedure for those wishing to complain about the handling of safeguarding issues.

Whistleblowing[15]

The diocese is available for advice and support on whistleblowing. This is when a paid church officer decides to pass on information concerning a wrong doing, that they consider is in the public interest. This means it must affect others, e.g. the general public. This includes failure to adhere to health and safety requirements that place others in danger, a 'cover up' by someone and/or a criminal offence. It does not cover personal grievance or complaints.

3. Abuse and Neglect of Children[16]

The abuse of children and young people can take many forms. They have the same right to protection regardless of age, disability, gender reassignment, race, religion or belief, sex, or sexual orientation. Children and young people from minority ethnic groups and those with disabilities (physical, sensory and/or learning difficulties) are especially vulnerable and need special care and protection.

Statutory definitions

The UK central government document 'Working Together to Safeguard Children' categorises and defines abuse in terms of:

- **Physical abuse** including hitting, shaking, throwing, poisoning, burning or scalding, drowning or suffocating.

- **Emotional abuse** including conveying to a child that they are inadequate, humiliation, blaming, controlling, intimidation, verbal abuse, isolation, seeing or hearing the ill-treatment of another. It may involve serious bullying (including cyberbullying).

- **Sexual abuse** including assault by penetration (for example, rape or oral sex) or non-penetrative acts such as masturbation, kissing, rubbing and touching outside of clothing. It may include involving children in looking at, or in the production of, sexual images, watching sexual activities, or grooming a child in preparation for abuse.

- **Neglect** including failure to provide adequate food, clothing and shelter, to protect a child from physical and emotional harm or danger, to provide adequate supervision and/or access to appropriate medical care or treatment. It may occur during pregnancy as a result of maternal substance abuse.

Domestic abuse

Witnessing domestic abuse is child abuse[17], and teenagers can suffer domestic abuse in their relationships.

Sexual exploitation

Child Sexual Exploitation (CSE) is a type of sexual abuse. Children or young people may be tricked into believing they are in a loving, consensual relationship. They might be invited to parties and given drugs and alcohol. They may also be groomed and exploited online. Some children and young people are trafficked into or within the UK for the purpose of sexual exploitation.

Bullying and cyberbullying

Bullying is behaviour that hurts someone else – such as name calling, hitting, pushing, spreading rumours, threatening or undermining someone. It can happen anywhere – at school, at home or online. It is usually repeated over a long period of time and can hurt a child both physically and emotionally. Bullying that happens online, using social networks, games and mobile phones, is often called cyberbullying. A child can feel like there is no escape because it can happen wherever they are, at any time of day or night.

Online abuse

With the ever-growing use of the internet, mobile telephones and online gaming (e.g. Xbox/ PlayStation), there has been a corresponding rise in the use of the internet and other electronic communication to target, groom and abuse children. Adults may target chat rooms, social networking sites, messaging services, mobile phones, online gaming sites and the internet generally. Children are particularly vulnerable to abuse by adults who pretend to be children of similar ages when online and who try to obtain images or engineer meetings.

Electronic images

The downloading, keeping or distributing of indecent images of children are all classified as sexual offences[18]. Such offences are sometimes referred to as non-contact sexual offences. However, it must be remembered that children will have been abused in the making of the images. The texting of sexual messages and photographs (sometimes referred to as 'sexting' – see Fact Sheet – Sexting❶) can be particularly problematic and abusive amongst children and young people.

4. Abuse and Neglect of Adults[19]

All adults, including vulnerable adults, have a fundamental human right to choose how and with whom they live, even if this appears to involve a degree of risk. They should be supported to make those choices, to live as independently as possible and treated with respect and dignity.

Who abuses adults?

Potentially anyone, adult or child, can be the abuser of an adult. Abuse will sometimes be deliberate, but it may also be an unintended consequence of ignorance or lack of awareness. Alternatively, it may arise from frustration or lack of support. The list can include:

- Relatives of the vulnerable person including husband, wife, partner, son or daughter. It will sometimes include a relative who is a main carer.

- Neighbours.

- Paid carers.

- Workers in places of worship.

- People who are themselves vulnerable and/or are users of a care service.

- Confidence tricksters who prey on people in their own homes or elsewhere.

Relatives who are main carers

Carers can experience considerable stress, exhaustion and frustration without respite or support. This can lead to unintended poor care or abuse. Relatives who are the main carers may also be subject to abuse by those for whom they are caring. This abuse is often endured for long periods and unreported[20].

Institutions

All people living in institutions are more likely to have a degree of vulnerability. The Care Quality Commission[21] in England has responsibility for inspecting and regulating the quality of care in institutions such as residential care homes, domiciliary care services and hospitals. In addition, the Local Government Ombudsman[22] deals with complaints that relate to adult social care. HM Inspectorate of Prisons[23] in England inspects prisons. Some members of the parish may be visiting adults in institutions – hospitals, prisons and residential homes. If, as part of these responsibilities, they have concerns about the care being given and/or the way that someone is being treated, the DSA should be contacted. You can also refer directly to the institution or raise concerns with the appropriate inspection and/or complaints body.

Definitions of adult abuse

The UK central government document 'Care and Support Statutory Guidance' categorises and defines adult abuse in terms of:

- **Physical abuse** including hitting, slapping, pushing, kicking, misuse of medication, restraint or inappropriate sanctions.

- **Sexual abuse** including rape and sexual assault or sexual acts to which the vulnerable adult has not consented or could not consent or was pressurised into consenting.

- **Psychological abuse** including emotional abuse, threats of harm or abandonment, deprivation of contact, humiliation, blaming, controlling, intimidation, coercion, harassment, verbal abuse, isolation or withdrawal from services or supportive networks.

- **Financial or material abuse** including theft, fraud, exploitation, pressure in connection with wills, property or inheritance or financial transactions, or the misuse or misappropriation of property, possessions or benefits.

- **Neglect or acts of omission** including ignoring medical or physical care needs, failure to provide access to appropriate health, social care or educational services, the withholding of the necessities of life, such as medication, adequate nutrition and heating.

- **Discriminatory abuse** including racist, sexist, based on a person's disability, and other forms of harassment, slurs or similar treatment.

- **Domestic abuse** that is usually a systematic, repeated and escalating pattern of behaviour, by which the abuser seeks to control, limit and humiliate, often behind closed doors.

- **Organisational abuse** including neglect and poor care practice within an institution or specific care setting such as a hospital or care home. This may range from one-off incidents to ongoing ill-treatment. It can be through neglect or poor professional practice as a result of the structure, policies, processes and practices within an organisation.

- **Modern slavery** including human trafficking; forced labour and domestic servitude; and traffickers and slave masters using whatever means they have at their disposal to coerce, deceive and force individuals into a life of abuse, servitude and inhumane treatment[24].

5. Safer Recruitment[25]

A key way of protecting children and adults from harm is to ensure the careful recruitment of those working with them. The House of Bishops' Safeguarding Policy states, '*The Church will select and vet all those with any responsibility related to children, young people and vulnerable adults within the Church*'.

The PCC is responsible for the appointment of those working with children, young people and vulnerable adults, paid or unpaid. Often the responsibility is delegated to the incumbent. At least two individuals (who could include the incumbent) must be responsible for recruitment. All those involved in recruitment must be capable and competent, trained in safer recruitment and able to keep personal matters confidential.

1. Job/role description Construct a clear and accurate job description and person specification, or for an unpaid role, a role outline, who set out what tasks and responsibilities the applicant will undertake, and the skills and experience required. This will include what level of DBS check is required.	Model Role Description for a PSO **ⓘ** DBS Eligibility **ⓘ** DBS Frequently Asked Questions **ⓘ**
2. Advertise Advertise unpaid roles within parish notices and paid roles more widely.	
3. Application form Ask all applicants to complete an application form for all paid roles (a Curriculum Vitae may be used for voluntary roles but an application form is good practice and is recommended). Always ask for, take up and check two references.	Model Application Form **ⓘ**

4. Confidential Declaration Form Ask all applicants to complete a Confidential Declaration Form.	Confidential Declaration Form ⓘ
6 Shortlist (paid posts) Shortlist, carefully examining the application forms. Identify any gaps in employment/personal history and ensure those shortlisted meet the requirements of the person specification. **Shortlist (unpaid posts)** Review any interest from volunteers and assess suitability against requirements.	
6. Interview Have a face-to-face interview (or informal discussion if unpaid) with pre-planned and clear questions to assess applicants' suitability for the role. Seek explanations for gaps in employment/personal history. It may also be appropriate to ask the individual to complete a test or presentation if applicable. Check identification and the Confidential Declaration Form (CDF).	Model Interview Questions ⓘ Model Reference Request Letter ⓘ
7. Offer the role Decide whom to offer the role to. This decision will be made by the interviewing panel. This is subject to completion of all checks to the satisfaction of the PCC. No role can commence until satisfactory checks have been completed.	
8. Checks Once the applicant has been offered the role, subject to satisfactory checks, ask the applicant to complete an enhanced Disclosure and Barring Service (DBS)	Model Reference Request Letter ⓘ

check application[26] (online or paper depending on the diocese's process). Any blemished DBS checks or information of concern on the CDF must be risk assessed by the DSA. Always check the applicants' two references. Please note if someone has either never lived in the UK or spent a period of time overseas (i.e. lived abroad), the person making the appointment should request an additional check and ask the applicant to obtain criminality information from the country where he/she was resident[27]. It is also recommended to undertake an occupational health check for paid roles where possible.	
9. Appoint Once all checks are satisfactory and support the interview decision, the person can be formally appointed. It is recommended to add an end date to unpaid roles. This can always be extended but helps set expectations for both parties.	**Model Appointment Letter** ⓘ
10. Probation period Have a period of probation[28] for any paid role (or a settling-in period for unpaid) and review throughout, as well as at the end of this period.	
11. Induct, train and support Induct new unpaid and paid workers. This should include expectations in relation to behaviour (a Code of Conduct[29]). Ensure supervision/support is in place and arrange for attendance on the Church of England safeguarding training (see section 6).	

6. Safeguarding Training[30]

The House of Bishops' Safeguarding Policy states that the Church *'will train and equip church officers to have the confidence and skills they need to care and support children, young people and vulnerable adults and to recognise and respond to abuse.'*

The Training and Development Framework outlines the core safeguarding training that is available from the diocese.

C0 – Basic awareness	Recommended for anyone who needs a basic level of awareness of safeguarding. This module is also a pre-requisite for attendance at any other core training module.
C1 – Foundation	Required for anyone who has safeguarding responsibilities/contact with children and/or vulnerable adults.
C2 – Leadership	Required for anyone who has safeguarding leadership responsibilities and/or leads activities involving children and/or vulnerable adults.
C3 – Clergy and lay ministers	Those holding a license, commission, authorisation, permission to officiate from a bishop, ordained or lay.
C4 – Senior staff	Senior staff who have key roles in safeguarding policy, strategy and practice.
C5 – Refresher	To be undertaken every three years by those who have completed C1, C2 or C3.

Who gets what training in the parish?[31]

Basic safeguarding awareness

CO is a basic safeguarding awareness course that can be completed by any member of the congregation, to improve their understanding of abuse and enable them to help build a culture of informed vigilance within the Church. It can be undertaken online at https://safeguardingtraining.cofeportal.org/login/index.php

However, it is recommended that the following roles are encouraged to complete it:

Vergers, servers, welcomers, caretakers, refreshment helpers, shop staff, sidespersons, flower arrangers, administrative staff, bell-ringers, choir members/music group members (including sound/AV).

Additional core training requirements

Role	CO	C1	C2	C3	C5
Incumbent and clergy, including those who hold PTO	✔	✘	✘	✔	✔
Licensed lay minsters e.g. readers	✔	✘	✘	✔	✔
Parish workers with children/vulnerable adults (paid or volunteer)	✔	✔	✘	✘	✔
Leaders/supervisors of work with children/vulnerable adults (paid or volunteer)	✔	✔	✔	✘	✔
Parish safeguarding officers	✔	✔	✔	✘	✔
Church operations managers	✔	✔	✘	✘	✔
Church wardens	✔	✔	✔	✘	✔
PCC members	✔	✘	✘	✘	✘
PCC safeguarding leads	✔	✔	✔	✘	✔
Youth and children's pastors (if not ordained or licensed)	✔	✔	✔	✘	✔
Music activity leaders/choir leaders	✔	✔	✔	✘	✔
Bell tower captains	✔	✔	✔	✘	✔

7. Responding Promptly to Every Safeguarding Concern or Allegation

7.1 Quick guide

Concern/allegation
You suspect or witness abuse, or someone discloses information about a safeguarding concern or allegation

Emergency – immediate
If a child or adult is in immediate danger or requires medical attention, call the police and/or social services immediately on 999

Non-emergency – within 24 hours
Record and report to the incumbent/PSO or activity leader. Agree who will inform the DSA

Record and report all information to the incumbent and PSO

Record and discuss with the DSA within 24 hours

The DSA will provide advice and guidance

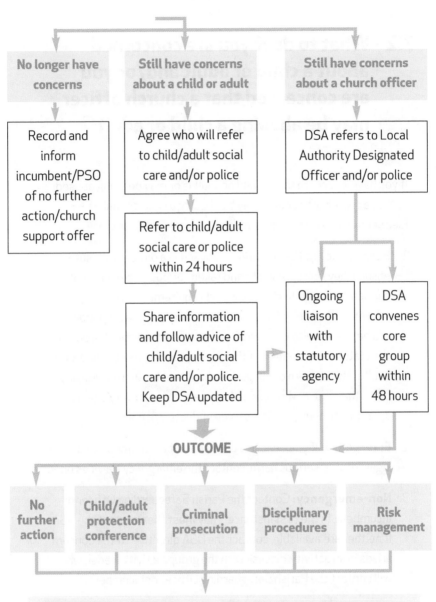

No longer have concerns	Still have concerns about a child or adult	Still have concerns about a church officer
Record and inform incumbent/PSO of no further action/church support offer	Agree who will refer to child/adult social care and/or police	DSA refers to Local Authority Designated Officer and/or police

Refer to child/adult social care or police within 24 hours

Share information and follow advice of child/adult social care and/or police. Keep DSA updated

Ongoing liaison with statutory agency

DSA convenes core group within 48 hours

OUTCOME

No further action	Child/adult protection conference	Criminal prosecution	Disciplinary procedures	Risk management

RECORD ALL ACTION – Consider the support needs of all those affected by allegations of abuse at all points in the above stages. Remember the safety and welfare of any child or adult takes precedence over all other concerns

7.2 What to do if you are concerned about a child or adult and/or you are concerned that a church officer[32] may be abusing a child or adult[33]

If you have a concern that a child or adult is or may be being abused, or that a church officer is or may be abusing a child or adult[34] (see sections 3 and 4 for information on types of abuse):

1. Respond well to the victim/survivor, if it is a direct disclosure, to ensure they feel listened to and taken seriously. Explain what will happen next and check out support requirements. They should be informed that their identity and the identity of the respondent[35] will be shared with key church officers[36], and may be shared with the statutory agencies[37], if there is any current risk to children or adults. The concern or allegation should not be shared with anyone other than those who need to know (e.g. the statutory agencies and appropriate church officers – see endnote 36) (see section 7.3).

2. **Emergency:** If you believe a child or adult is in immediate danger of significant or serious harm, contact the emergency services on 999.

3. **Non-emergency:** Contact the Parish Safeguarding Officer or incumbent, in the first instance. They **must** then contact the DSA. If neither are available, contact the DSA directly[38]. If the concern arises in an activity, discuss with the group/activity leader, who will contact the Parish Safeguarding Officer or incumbent.

4. Any safeguarding concerns **must** be reported to the DSA **within 24 hours**.

5. If the PSO/incumbent or the DSA are not available within 24 hours, contact Children's Social Care or Adult Social Care[39] and/or the police directly, if the concern is that a child or adult is being abused. Contact the Local Authority Designated Officer (LADO)[40] and/or police if the concern is that a church officer may be abusing a child or adult.

    Advise the Parish Safeguarding Officer or incumbent as soon as possible that you have made a referral; they will advise the DSA.

    If in doubt don't delay – seek advice from statutory agencies.

6. Do not contact the respondent[41] or anyone who may be implicated in the allegation or disclosure, even if they would normally be contacted as part of the procedure, until advice has been sought from the DSA or statutory agencies[42].

7. Record the details of the concern or allegation. Where it is not appropriate to take notes at the time (usually it will not be), make a written record as soon as possible afterwards or before the end of the day. Record the time, date, location, persons present and how the concern or allegation was received, e.g. by telephone, face-to-face conversation, letter, etc. The record should include details of information provided to that person as well as the information received. Always sign and date the record. Keep it factual. Pass on a copy to the DSA (and/or the PSO/incumbent). The records should be kept secure and confidential (please see Model Parish Recording Template ❶).

If the concern is about a child or adult:

8. The DSA will act in line with the House of Bishops' guidance. They will offer advice, support and guidance and help to make

the required referrals. If there is a risk of harm, the concerns must be reported to the statutory agencies within 24 hours of the DSA receiving the concerns. This would be Children's or Adult Social Care and/or the police.

There should be close communication between the DSA and PSO/incumbent until the situation is resolved. The archdeacon should also be informed.

If the concern also involves a church officer:

9. The DSA will act in line with the House of Bishops' guidance. They will offer advice, support and guidance and refer the concerns to the Local Authority Designated Officer (LADO) and/or police within 24 hours. The DSA will now take over the management of the safeguarding concern in conjunction with the core group (which will be convened within 48 hours) and statutory agencies. There may also be a requirement for parish representatives to attend a subsequent core group/s. If there are doubts about whether or not to make a referral and under what route, the DSA will seek advice from the LADO.

Please note that the procedure is the same for non-recent abuse[43].

A proper balance must be struck between protecting children and adults, and respecting the rights of the person against whom an allegation is made. In such circumstances the welfare of the child, young person or adult must come first. The rights of the person against whom the allegation is made are important and must be given due weight, once the immediate safety and protection of the child, young person or vulnerable adult have been assured.

7.3 Guidelines for responding to a person disclosing abuse

Respond

Do:

- Listen.
- Take what is said seriously.
- Only use open questions (open questions begin with words like: who, what, when, where and how. Open questions cannot be answered with a 'yes' or 'no').
- Remain calm.
- Take into account the person's age and level of understanding.
- Check, if face to face, whether they mind you taking notes while they talk so you can make sure you capture the information accurately. At the end you can check with them that you have understood everything correctly.
- Offer reassurance that disclosing is the right thing to do.
- Establish only as much information as is needed to be able to tell your activity leader / Parish Safeguarding Officer / DSA and statutory authorities what is believed to have happened, when and where.
- Check what the person hopes to happen as a result of the disclosure.
- Tell the child or adult what you are going to do next.

Do not:

- Make promises that cannot be kept (e.g. that you won't share the information).
- Make assumptions or offer alternative explanations.
- Investigate.
- Contact the person about whom allegations have been made.
- Do a physical or medical examination.

Record

- Make some very brief notes at the time, if appropriate, and write them up in detail as soon as possible.
- Do not destroy your original notes in case they are required by the DSA or the statutory authorities.
- Record the date, time, place and actual words used, including any swear words or slang.
- Record facts and observable things, not your interpretations or assumptions.
- Don't speculate or jump to conclusions.

Report

- If there is immediate danger to a child or adult contact the police.
- Otherwise report to your activity leader/Parish Safeguarding Officer/incumbent immediately.
- Within 24 hours the PSO/incumbent reports the concerns to the DSA.
- The DSA will advise regarding reporting to statutory agencies within 24 hours.
- If there is any doubt seek advice from Children's/Adult's Social Care or the police.

7.4 Non-recent abuse

Safeguarding concerns or allegations may be about something that is going on now and/or something that may happen in the future (recent) or something that happened in the past (non-recent). Non-recent allegations of abuse must be treated as seriously as recent allegations. Research evidences that it may take up to 25 years or longer for an adult to disclose sexual abuse that happened to him/her either as a child or younger adult. A victim/survivor needs to be aware that if a respondent is known to be currently working with children/vulnerable adults in either a paid or voluntary capacity a referral to the statutory services will be made. The DSA will make this referral[44].

7.5 Domestic abuse[45]

The House of Bishops' policy states that 'The Church is committed to those who have been victims and survivors of domestic abuse. Domestic abuse in all its forms is contrary to the will of God and an affront to human dignity. All need to play their part in preventing or halting it'. The welfare of the adult victim of domestic abuse is important, but where there are children in the family it must be understood that they too are victims of domestic abuse. Consideration of the child's welfare always comes first. In all circumstances, contact the DSA who will help clarify the issues and steps needed, which may involve contacting Children's Social Care. There may be a need for a risk assessment and for a Safeguarding Agreement ⓘ to be put in place. The DSA will undertake this work in conjunction with the parish church and any statutory agencies (see section 10).

What do you need to do in a parish?

- PCC to agree a parish domestic abuse statement including who to contact if there are concerns.

- Appoint a named individual who is a point of contact for any advice and support. This may be the Parish Safeguarding Officer (PSO).

- Follow the process on how to respond to safeguarding concerns or allegations.

- Support those in leadership positions, pastoral and safeguarding roles to engage in diocesan domestic abuse training.

- Consider the best place to display the domestic abuse statement including information about helplines and local services.

- Discuss domestic abuse in appropriate contexts such as marriage preparation.

- Challenge inappropriate comments and behaviour by church members.

Recommended good practice:

- Encourage leaders and those who preach to speak against domestic abuse in teaching, sermons, prayers and parish magazines – remember that many of the congregation may have personal experience of domestic abuse.

- Offer some awareness-raising activities e.g. invite speakers from local domestic abuse agencies.

- Consider including activities around healthy relationships within activities for children and young people.

- Develop links with local domestic abuse organisations.

- Organise courses in parenting and confidence-building.

7.6   Ministry of deliverance

Concerns may be expressed that a child, young person or adult is troubled by or possessed by evil spirits or demons and that this may account for behavioural issues in the individual or be considered to justify harsh treatment by the family, guardians, friends or carers.

If a church officer, including a member of clergy, becomes aware of the above situation and/or a request is made for deliverance ministry, the parish **must** contact the **DSA** who will contact the appropriate person.

7.7   Recording, data protection and information sharing

Opening a church safeguarding case file

Good record keeping is an important part of the safeguarding task. A record, called a case file, should be opened whenever a safeguarding concern or allegation occurs in a church. The record should include key contact details, dates of when the information became known and the nature of the concerns. The record should include ongoing actions with dates, other key documents on the case file (e.g. observation notes, reports, consent forms etc.) and the case closure date. Records should use straightforward language and be concise and accurate so that they can be understood by anyone not familiar with the case. Please see Model Parish Recording Template ❶.

Record retention and security

The safeguarding case files, whether electronic or paper, must be stored securely by the incumbent and the PSO. This should include identifying who should have access to them. Records in relation to safeguarding issues, even if they have not been proven, should be maintained in accordance with the Church's retention guidance. If the incumbent moves from the church, the records should be passed to the new incumbent.

Data protection and information sharing

In May 2018, the General Data Protection Regulation (GDPR) and the Data Protection Act 2018 replaced the Data Protection Act 1998. The GDPR contains the principles governing the use of personal data. It should be noted that the GDPR and the Data Protection Act 2018 place greater significance on organisations being accountable and transparent in relation to their use of personal data. Parishes handling personal data need to have the proper arrangements for collecting, storing and sharing information[46].

Personal information in relation to safeguarding will often be sensitive and is likely to be classed as what is called 'special categories of personal data' under the GDPR, which means extra care will need to be taken when handling such data. Nevertheless, it is important to be aware that the Data Protection Act 2018 includes specific reference to processing data in relation to the 'safeguarding of children and individuals at risk' and allows individuals to share, in certain situations, personal data without consent (see below)[47].

'*The GDPR and Data Protection Act 2018 do not prevent, or limit, the sharing of information for the purposes of keeping children and young people safe*' and this can equally be said to apply to vulnerable adults[48].

Reporting concerns about adults

Referrals of suspected abuse are made to Adult Social Services and the police. Where possible, for a person over 18, this should be done with their written consent.

The starting point is the presumption that an adult can give consent and has the mental capacity to do so. The provisions of the Mental Capacity Act 2005 are complex and questions and concerns about consent and mental capacity should always be discussed with the DSA.

Sharing without consent

Information can be shared legally without consent, if a person is unable to or cannot reasonably be expected to gain consent from the individual concerned, or if to gain consent could place somebody at risk. Relevant personal data can be shared lawfully without consent if it is to keep a child or vulnerable adult safe from neglect or physical, emotional or mental harm, or if it is protecting their physical, mental or emotional well-being.

Never make these decisions on your own. If you are going to share personal data, this should always be discussed with the DSA. Of course, you may be able to share data, at least initially, without identifying the individual concerned both within the church and with the statutory services.

Ultimately, the most important consideration is whether the sharing of information is likely to support the safeguarding of a child, young person or vulnerable adult.

8. Caring Pastorally for Victims/Survivors of Abuse and Affected Others

The House of Bishops' Safeguarding Policy 2017 states that
'The Church will endeavour to offer care and support to all those that have been abused, regardless of the type of abuse, when or where it occurred …Those who have suffered abuse within the Church will receive a compassionate response, be listened to and be taken seriously. Our first response to those who have suffered abuse, especially abuse within the Church, should be compassionate; we must listen and take what we are hearing seriously.'

Most parishes are likely to have amongst their congregation children and young people who have been abused and/or adults who have experienced abuse, either as adults or when they themselves were children. Some may have been abused in the Church (see below).

Responding well to a disclosure of abuse is essential to being able to build trust and support (see section 7.3). For some, just being able to talk to a trusted person about their experiences can be a powerful, healing event. Some may be seeking pastoral support from the Church. Some may need advice about how best to seek professional help. This may involve support to access local specialist services. Victims/survivors who are children or young people will require specialist support. If you need any advice about how best to support a victim/survivor of abuse, please contact the DSA.

We journey alongside those who have been abused; for some, forgiveness may be a part of that journey, while for others, it may not be so. In any event, there should not be any pressure or expectation from the church on the victim/survivor to forgive[49].

Support following alleged abuse by a church officer

All concerns or allegations of abuse by a church officer must be reported to the DSA (see section 7.2). The DSA will arrange for a **Support Person** to be offered to all alleged adult victims/survivors. The role of the Support Person is set out in the House of Bishops' guidance[50]. What the Support Person offers will be agreed with the alleged victim/survivor, but it is likely they will:

- Listen to and represent the victim/survivor's pastoral needs.

- Identify any therapeutic or other needs and offer choices as to how these best be met.

- Record any meetings or contact they have with the victim/survivor.

- Share relevant information with the DSA.

Victims/survivors who are children or young people will require specialist support. The DSA will seek advice from Children's Social Care to access support from a professional agency, as required.

Support for families of victims/survivors and for the parish is co-ordinated by the core group in conjunction with statutory agencies. This would involve discussion with the Parish Safeguarding Officer, incumbent and archdeacon as appropriate.

In addition, dioceses have access to specialist support services for victims/survivors of abuse. This may be through a Diocesan Authorised Listener or a commissioned external service. The nature of any ongoing support needs will be agreed by the DSA with the victim/survivor[51].

9. Caring Pastorally for Church Officers who are the Subject of Concerns or Allegations of Abuse and Affected Others

9.1 Support for the respondent[52]

Support for the respondent is provided by a **Link Person**. All church officers who are the subject of a concern will be offered a Link Person.

The statutory agencies, where involved, will inform the DSA about when and what they can tell the respondent about an allegation that has been made. It may be that the statutory agencies themselves inform the respondent as part of their own investigative practices i.e. where a voluntary interview or arrest is necessary.

Where the statutory agencies are not involved, the core group will determine when and what the respondent should be told. This will normally be done by the diocesan bishop's nominated representative and the DSA, at an arranged meeting with the respondent. At this meeting the respondent will also be offered a Link Person and the support needs of the respondent's family will be considered.

The role of the Link Person is set out in the House of Bishops' guidance[53]. What the Link Person offers will be agreed with the respondent, but it is likely he/she will:

- Keep the person up to date with the progress of their case.

- Help with access to advice and additional support.

- Make and keep a written record of any meetings or contact with the respondent and share relevant information with the DSA.

For clergy or lay workers whose accommodation is provided by the Church, alternative temporary accommodation for the respondent may need to be considered by the diocese.

9.2 Support to parishes and others affected by safeguarding concerns or allegations

When a member of clergy leaves a parish in which they have lived and worked for some time, there is usually a period of notice during which they can take their leave and parishioners can say their goodbyes. The pastoral relationship between the respondent and parishioners can be very close, so when it is ending it is to be expected that there will be some sense of loss and sadness; but there is also an opportunity to mark their departure.

When someone in a position of office or ministry must step aside at short notice or is suspended because of a safeguarding concern or allegation, a crisis arises for them, but also for the parishioners who have had no warning. The feelings that can arise for parishioners in these circumstances can be very varied and can include disbelief about the allegation, defensiveness about the respondent, shock, disappointment, anger and confusion. People can feel abandoned, especially if they had been working closely with that person in some element of parish life.

The core group will advise the DSA, in close liaison with the archdeacon, who should support the affected parish.

During the period of investigation, which may last for many months, the information that can be shared with the parish and its congregation will be limited. Advice and support are available from the DSA, the archdeacon and the Diocesan Communications Officer.

10. Responding to Those who May Present a Known Risk to Children, Young People or Vulnerable Adults within a Christian Congregation[54]

The House of Bishops' Safeguarding Policy 2017 states, *'The Church, based on the message of the gospel, opens its doors to all. It will therefore endeavour to offer pastoral care and support to any member of the church community whom may present a known risk.'*

This means that there are likely to be those with criminal convictions for sexual offences and other forms of abuse attending church. In addition, there may be those who do not have convictions or cautions but where there are sound reasons for considering that they still might pose a risk to others. Where people may pose a risk to others, their position in a congregation will need to be carefully and sensitively assessed to decide whether they pose a present risk to others and to put in place arrangements to ensure that these risks are mitigated. In these circumstances it is not only about monitoring individuals but offering support to lead a fulfilled life. As such, the Church has an important role in contributing to the prevention of future abuse.

Some examples of the risk that individuals may pose to children, young people and adults are:

- **Sexual offences – against both adults and children**: this includes accessing indecent images of children on the internet.

- **Financial abuse**: targeting of vulnerable adults for financial gain, for example, asking for money, the acceptance of large 'gifts' or offering to do a job for someone at an extortionate rate of pay.

Take action

Always contact the DSA as soon as practicable, but within 24 hours, if you learn that any of the following people worship in your church:

1. Anyone placed on the sex offenders register, with a violent offence or conviction and/or who is barred from working with children or adults by the Disclosure and Barring Service.

2. Anyone who admits to being an abuser including non-recent abuse.

3. Anyone who is subject to an investigation for suspected abuse, including possession of indecent images of children, and/or is suspended from their usual role.

4. Anyone who may pose a risk to other church members due to their behaviour, irrespective of their criminal status.

Category (4) may include a person in relation to whom:

- An allegation of abuse against a child or adult has been investigated, but the matter has not proceeded to court, or the person has been acquitted, or the matter is currently the subject of proceedings in the criminal or civil courts but the person may still pose a risk.

- A complaint or grievance has been received alleging inappropriate behaviour, which is not criminal.

- There have been concerns about the person's alleged abusive behaviour to a previous or current partner.

If the DSA is made aware by any other source of any person in the above categories who is intending to or is worshipping at a local parish church, he/she will notify the Parish Safeguarding Officer/incumbent in the first instance.

The DSA will determine the appropriate action to be taken to best safeguard the parish and its congregation, based on the particular facts and circumstances of each case. They will undertake a risk assessment and the formation of a risk management plan known as a Safeguarding Agreement ❶.

This will involve the respondent and usually the incumbent, church warden, Parish Safeguarding Officer and, if involved, statutory agencies e.g. police, National Probation Service and Children's Social Care. Who is involved will depend on the case.

If a person is assessed as posing a risk to children or adults, the DSA, together with any statutory agencies involved, will support the parish to:

- Form a small group of people to offer pastoral support, friendship and to monitor the respondent.

- Maintain the highest levels of confidentiality unless there is a breach of the agreement and it is necessary to inform others to protect a child or vulnerable adult.

- Agree with the respondent that he/she worship elsewhere if his/her victim or their family worship in the same church.

- Ensure the respondent is never offered any official role in the church or position of responsibility where he/she may be trusted by others, for example that of church warden, worship leader or any in which a child or vulnerable adult may, as a result, place trust in that person.

- Consider whether, with the person's agreement and that of any statutory authorities involved, the congregation should be informed.

- Meet with the respondent to draft a Safeguarding Agreement ⓘ, setting out the parameters of his/her behaviour in the church setting.

The Safeguarding Agreement may include the following elements:

- Attend designated services or meetings only.

- Sit apart from children.

- Stay away from areas of the building where children or vulnerable adults meet.

- Attend a house group where there are no children or vulnerable adults.

- Decline hospitality where there are children or vulnerable adults.

- Never be alone with children or vulnerable adults.

- Never work or be part of a mixed group with children or vulnerable adults.

- Take no role or office in the church which gives him or her status or authority as others may deem that person to be trustworthy.

The church wardens should be involved in the drawing up of the written agreement with the respondent. Church wardens can direct parishioners where to sit and have a duty to maintain good order at divine service. If necessary church wardens can eject a person creating a disturbance and in certain circumstances have the power of arrest, although such power should be exercised with extreme caution[55]. If a 'disturbance' is anticipated the police must be notified.

The Safeguarding Agreement will be monitored and reviewed at least annually.

Should the respondent refuse to sign the agreement the DSA will advise the parish and liaise with the police and other relevant agencies, as required, to seek a resolution. Any breach should be shared with the DSA immediately, who will liaise with the statutory agencies, as required. It should be remembered that it is not possible to prevent a parishioner from attending divine service[56], unless this is a condition included in a court order or in his/her licence conditions upon release from prison (although, of course, he/she could voluntarily agree not to attend certain services). If a respondent parishioner wishes to attend any service, as part of the safeguarding arrangement (and this could be contained in his/her ongoing Safeguarding Agreement), it is possible for the church wardens to direct a person where to sit, put measures in place to closely supervise them (e.g. accompany the individual) and remove that person if they cause a disturbance. It is also possible to refuse access to other church activities (e.g. social activities such as tea/coffee after the service and choir and bell ringing activities).

11. A Safe Environment and Activities[57]

The House of Bishops' Safeguarding Policy Statement states that
*'The Church will strive to create and maintain environments that are
safer for all, that promote well-being, that prevent abuse, and that create
nurturing, caring conditions within the Church for children, young people
and vulnerable adults … The Church will strive to support all church
officers to adhere to safer working good practice and to challenge
the abuse of power'.*

11.1 Code of safer working practice[58]

**All those working on behalf of the parish with children, young
people and adults must:**

- Treat all individuals with respect and dignity.

- Ensure that their own language, tone of voice and body language
  are respectful.

- Ensure that children, young people and adults know who they can
  talk to about a personal concern.

- Record and report any concerns about a child, young person or adult
  and/or the behaviour of another worker with their activity leader
  and/or Parish Safeguarding Officer. Sign and date the record.

- Obtain written consent for any photographs/videos to be taken,
  shown, displayed or stored (see Model Consent Form –
  Photographs – Images ⓘ).

- Administer any First Aid with others around.

In addition, for children and young people must:

- Always aim to work with or within sight of another adult.

- Ensure another adult is informed if a child needs to be taken to the toilet. Toilet breaks should be organised for young children.

- Respond warmly to a child who needs comforting but make sure there are other adults around.

- Ensure that the child and parents are aware of any activity that requires physical contact and its nature before the activity takes place.

All those working on behalf of the parish with children, young people and adults must not:

- Invade an individual's privacy whilst washing and toileting.

- Use any form of physical punishment.

- Be sexually suggestive about or to an individual.

- Scapegoat, ridicule or reject an individual or group.

- Permit abusive peer activities e.g. initiation ceremonies, ridiculing or bullying.

- Show favoritism to any one individual or group.

- Allow an individual to involve you in excessive attention seeking.

- Allow unknown adults access to children, young people and adults who may be vulnerable. Visitors should always be accompanied by an approved person.

- Allow strangers to give children, young people and adults who may be vulnerable in the group, lifts.

- Befriend children, young people and adults who may be vulnerable on social media.

- Take photographs on personal phones or cameras as this means that images are stored on personal devices.

In addition, for children and young people, must not:

- Give lifts to children you are supervising, on their own or your own (unless there are exceptional circumstances e.g. in an emergency for medical reasons or where parents fail to collect a child and no other arrangements can be made to take a child home. In such situations, the circumstances and your decision must be recorded and shared with an appropriate person at the earliest opportunity).

- Smoke or drink alcohol in the presence of children and young people.

- Arrange social occasions with children and young people (other than events which also include adult family members/carers) outside organised group occasions.

11.2 Acceptable touch

Sympathetic attention, humour, encouragement and appropriate physical contact are needed by children and adults. Some physical contact with children, particularly younger children, is wholly appropriate. The following guidelines regarding touching are suggested:

- **Always** ask permission.

- Be mindful of your body position.

- Keep everything public. A hug in the context of a group is very different from a hug behind closed doors.

- Touch should be in response to a child's needs and not related to the worker's needs. It should be age appropriate, welcome and generally initiated by the child, not the church officer.

- Avoid any physical contact that is or could be construed as sexual and/or abusive/offensive.

- Allow the child to determine the degree of physical contact with others except in exceptional circumstances (e.g. when they need medical attention).

In addition:

- ✓ You can allow people you support to give you brief hugs if you feel comfortable with this.

- ✓ You can allow people you support to hold hands or link arms with you to help with travel and stability.

- ✓ You should discourage people you support from touching your face. You can offer your hand instead.

- ✓ You should discourage people you support from sitting on your lap. You can offer to sit side by side.

✓ You should avoid using touch if the person you support is very distressed and is unlikely to tolerate it.

Ensure that church officers at all levels must take responsibility for monitoring one another in the area of physical contact. They should be encouraged to challenge one another if necessary. Concerns about possible abuse or inappropriate behaviour should always be reported.

11.3 Children's activities

Church groups that involve children need to ensure good practice standards across a wide range of areas including: recruitment of activity leaders; DBS checking; staffing ratios; suitability of premises; health and safety arrangements; and facilities for children with special needs.

The minimum staffing levels for groups should be as follows[59]:

0 – 2 years	1 adult to 3 children	1:3
2 – 3 years	1 adult to 4 children	1:4
4 – 8 years	1 adult to 6 children	1:6
9 – 12 years	1 adult to 8 children	1:8
13 – 18 years	1 adult to 10 children	1:10

Each group should have at least two workers, even for smaller groups, and if possible one male and one female. Staff ratios for all groups should always be based on a risk assessment. For example, staffing numbers would need to be increased for outdoor activities and more so if that activity is considered higher risk, potentially dangerous or when children with disabilities or special needs are involved.

For all groups and activities:

- Undertake a health and safety risk assessment (see Model Activity Risk Assessment Template 🛈).

- A registration form[60] must be completed for every child or young person who attends groups or activities which should include up-to- date information on parents' contact numbers, medical information (e.g. allergies) and any special needs (see Model Registration Form – Activities and Trips 🛈).

- An attendance register must be kept and be available at all group meetings.

- A First Aid kit must be available on any premises that are used by children.

- An accident and incident logbook must be available, and all accidents recorded. The logbook should be stored in a secure place. Any significant incidents must be recorded (e.g. a fight between children).

- There should be access to a telephone, if possible.

- In premises where children's groups meet, the Childline and Family Lives telephone numbers should be displayed (see section 13).

- Parents must sign a consent form before children are transported in a private car, and before any photography or images are taken (see Model Consent Form – Transport 🛈).

In addition, when taking children offsite[61]:

- The church leadership must be informed and agree to the activity.

- Details of the activity and any itinerary must be given in advance to parent/s and consent forms received in advance of the activity taking place.

- Details of the activity and a list of contacts must be left with someone in the church.

- Details of the activity and arrangements must be given to the incumbent and/or PSO.

- A risk assessment must be undertaken, and confirmation obtained that the activity is covered by PCC insurance.

- A leader must be designated to take responsibility for First Aid.

Many of these items are equally applicable to groups involving vulnerable adults.

11.4 Visiting adults

Visiting vulnerable adults in their homes is an essential element of many church officers' roles. Many parishioners will be well known to the church officer and where there have been no previous concerns, the level of risk to the church officer or parishioner during visits will usually be low. However, unexpected circumstances can be encountered, some of which may place a church officer at risk. For example, the unexpected presence in the home of a relative or friend with a history of violence or threatening behaviour. Unfortunately, case histories also show that a parishioner may be at risk from a church officer. For these reasons it is very important for parishes to ensure their church officers and parishioners are as safe as they can be, and that there is accountability and transparency in the manner in which church officers engage in lone working or visits to homes.

To assure the person you are visiting of their safety, and for your own as a church officer:

- If possible undertake a risk assessment before an initial visit, especially if you do not know the person. If there are any concerns or risks known before a visit is made, you are advised always to undertake a risk assessment (see Model Risk Assessment Checklist for Home Visiting ❶). In these circumstances, consider whether the visit is necessary, or whether you should be accompanied by another church officer. In addition, visiting in pairs may be advisable, especially if the adult is perceived to be vulnerable.

- Do not call unannounced; call by appointment, if appropriate telephoning the person just before visiting.

- Be clear about what support you can offer and the purpose and limitations of any pastoral care/support that is available.

- Do not make referrals to any agency that could provide help without the adult's permission, and ideally encourage them to set up the contact, unless there are safeguarding concerns.

- Never offer 'over-the-counter' remedies to people on visits or administer prescribed medicines, even if asked to do so.

- Do not accept any gifts from adults other than token items, to avoid misunderstandings or subsequent accusations from the person or their family. If someone wants to make a donation to the church, put it in an envelope, mark it on the outside as a donation and obtain a receipt from the Treasurer.

- Make a note of the date when you visit people, report back about the visit to the agreed named person and say what is concerning or going well. They will report safeguarding concerns to the Parish Safeguarding Officer and/or incumbent or directly to the DSA if they are not available.

12.   Use of Social Media

Social media sites enable users to create and share content and keep in touch with other users. They include maintaining a profile on a networking site such as Facebook, Twitter, Instagram, Snapchat; writing or commenting on a blog, whether it is your own or the blog of another person; and taking part in discussions on web forums or message boards. For many, especially young people, using social media is an extension of physical face-to-face relationships. It is therefore important that churches also engage with their community and worshippers through these platforms. However, this must be done safely to avoid the risk of:

- Forming inappropriate relationships.
- Saying things you should not, such as offensive, sexual or suggestive comments.
- Blurring the boundaries between public work/ministry and your private life.
- Grooming and impersonation.
- Bullying and harassment.

The role of the PCC

The PCC must approve the use of social media and mobile phones by the church. Where there are Facebook or similar online groups set up on the church's behalf, the PCC must ensure there is a **named person** to whom all workers are accountable.

The named person must be a church officer, and should be aware of the account name and password so that they can at any time log on to the account to monitor the communications. The named person should be proactive in fulfilling this role.

Communications must be shared with the named person. Church officers remain bound by professional rules of confidentiality. Where there is concern that a young person or adult is at risk of abuse, or they themselves pose a risk of abuse to others, safeguarding procedures must always be followed.

Guidance for church officers

Do:

✓ Have your eyes open and be vigilant.

✓ Maintain the upmost integrity – honesty, transparency, consistency and accountability are key. Treat online communication with children, young people and adults as you would communication that is face to face. Always maintain the same level of confidentiality.

✓ Report any safeguarding concerns that arise on social media to the PSO and the DSA.

✓ Always assume that everything you write is permanent and may be viewed by anyone at any time; and that everything can be traced back to you personally as well as to your colleagues or the church. Always think before you post.

✓ Draw clear boundaries around your social media usage associated with your private life and your use of different social media for public ministry. Keep church account/s and profiles separate from your personal social media account/s e.g. only use a Facebook page, Twitter or blogs for public ministry, while keeping a separate Facebook profile for private life.

✓ Always ask parents/carers for written consent to:

- Use and store photographs of children/young people from activities or events in official church publications, or on the church's social media, website and displays.

- Use telephone, text message, email and other messaging services to communicate with young people.

- Allow young people to connect to the church's social media pages.

✓ Only use an approved church/ministry account to communicate with children, young people and/or vulnerable adults. The named person should be able to access this and review conversations, and the account should be visible to young people and their parents. Young people must be made aware that any communication will be viewed by all users. Save any messages and threads through social networking sites, so that you can provide evidence to the named person of your exchange when required.

✓ Avoid one-to-one communication with a child or young person.

✓ Use clear and unambiguous language in all communications and avoid abbreviations that could be misinterpreted.

✓ Save and download to hard copy any inappropriate material received through social networking sites or other electronic means and show immediately to the named person, PSO, incumbent or, if appropriate, Diocesan Safeguarding Adviser.

✓ Use passwords and log off promptly after use to ensure that nobody else can use social media pretending to be you.

Do not:

➢ Use a personal Facebook or any other social media account in your work with children, young people or vulnerable adults.

➢ Add children, young people or vulnerable adults as friends on your personal accounts.

➢ Facebook stalk (i.e. dig through people's Facebook pages to find out about them).

➢ Say anything on social media that you would not be happy saying in a public meeting, to someone's face, writing in a local newspaper or on headed notepaper.

➢ Comment on photos or posts, or share content, unless appropriate to your church role.

➢ Use visual media (e.g. Skype, Facetime) for one-to-one conversations with young people – use only in group settings.

In particular, do not allow content to contain or share links to other sites that contain:

➢ Libellous, defamatory, bullying or harassing statements.

➢ Breaches of copyright and data protection.

➢ Material of an illegal nature.

➢ Offensive sexual or abusive references.

➢ Inappropriate language.

➢ Anything which may be harmful to a child, young person or vulnerable adult, or which may bring the church into disrepute or compromise its reputation.

Mobile phones

Wherever possible, church officers should be supplied with a mobile phone dedicated for work purposes. This allows for the phone to be switched off outside working hours, and for usage to be accountable. This means that the work phone number is the only number that young people or adults are given, and the church officer's personal number can remain private. Texts or conversations that raise concerns should be saved and passed on to the named person or the PSO/incumbent (or if unavailable the DSA).

13. Further Help and Guidance

Helplines

NSPCC for adults concerned about a child – **0808 800 5000**

Childline for children and young people – **0800 1111**

Action on Elder Abuse helpline – **0808 808 8141**

24-hour National Domestic Violence helpline – 0808 2000 247

NAPAC offers support and advice to adult survivors of childhood abuse – 08088010331

Stop It Now helps prevent child sexual abuse – **0808 1000 900**

Cruse bereavement helpline – **0808 808 1677**

Family Lives provides support and advice on family issues – **0808 800 222**

MACSAS for people who have been abused by church officers – **0808 801 0340**

Samaritans for people struggling to cope and needing someone to talk to – 116 123

Sources of support for victims and families of abuse

The Survivors Trust – http://thesurvivorstrust.org

Safeline – www.safeline.org.uk/what-can-friends-and-family-members-do-to-support-survivors-of-sexual-abuse

SupportLine – www.supportline.org.uk/problems/rape_sexual-assault.php

Victim Support – www.victimsupport.org.uk/crime-info/types-crime/childhood-abuse

Websites

www.nspcc.org.uk

www.womensaid.org.uk

www.restoredrelationships.org

www.stopitnow.org.uk

www.scie.org.uk

www.ceop.police.uk

www.elderabuse.org.uk

www.ageuk.org.uk

www.barnardos.org.uk

www.spiritualabuse.com

www.modernslavery.co.uk

https://carers.org

For links to the resources and templates mentioned in this handbook, go to www.churchofengland.org/safeguarding

All House of Bishops' Safeguarding Policy and Guidance can be found at www.churchofengland.org/more/safeguarding/policy-practice-guidance

In addition, please see the safeguarding pages of your diocesan website.

Appendix – Further Information on Vulnerable Adults

The term **'vulnerable adult'** refers to a person aged 18 or over whose ability to protect himself or herself from violence, abuse, neglect or exploitation is significantly impaired through physical or mental disability, illness, old age, emotional fragility, distress, or otherwise; and for that purpose, the reference to being impaired is to being temporarily or indefinitely impaired[62].

Please note that some adults may not consider themselves vulnerable but may be vulnerable to being abused by individuals in positions of leadership and responsibility. As adults are not inherently vulnerable and in need of protection it is important to recognise that the factors described below do not, of themselves, mean that a person is vulnerable. It is a combination of these factors and the circumstances that a person finds him/herself in that can make an individual vulnerable to abuse or neglect.

Some factors that increase vulnerability include:	
<ul><li>A mental illness, chronic or acute.</li><li>A sensory or physical disability or impairment.</li><li>A learning disability.</li><li>A physical illness.</li><li>Dementia.</li><li>An addiction to alcohol or drugs.</li><li>Failing faculties of old age.</li><li>Those who are homeless.</li><li>Refugee families or individuals (including those seeking asylum).</li></ul>	<ul><li>Victims/survivors of domestic abuse – direct violence and/or significant emotional coercion.</li><li>Those who have suffered historic abuse in childhood.</li><li>A permanent or temporary reduction in physical, mental or emotional capacity brought about by life events – for example bereavement or abuse or trauma.</li></ul>
These factors may not exist in isolation; for example, someone with a drink problem masking underlying dementia; or a frail housebound elderly person with underlying depression.	

Notes

Introduction

1. The term 'child' is used to include all children and young people who have not yet reached their 18th birthday. The fact that a child has reached 16 years of age, is living independently, is in further education, is a member of the armed forces, in hospital, in prison or in a Young Offender's institution does not change his or her status or entitlement to services or protection under the Children Act 1989. The handbook also uses the term 'young person/people' for those aged between 14 and 17.

2. Please note that these may be the same person.

3. This means that the 'relevant persons' as defined in the 2016 Measure (who include but are not limited to the incumbent, the PCC and the church wardens) will need to comply with its terms unless they can point to cogent reasons for not doing so (to be 'cogent', such reasons must be clear, logical and convincing).

1. Parish Roles and Responsibilities

4. For further information, please see section 3 in the House of Bishops' Key Roles and Responsibilities of Church Office Holders and Bodies Practice Guidance (Roles 2017).

5. Church wardens operate in accordance with the Church Wardens Measure 2001 and the Canons of the Church of England (see Canon E1 in particular). Their safeguarding responsibilities are outlined in section 3 of Roles 2017.

6. In addition, the diocese may offer an aligned parish safeguarding policy bespoke for its parishes.

7. Section 3.3 of Roles 2017 states that '*Preferably the PSO should be someone who is a lay person, has good pastoral and organisational skills and experience of working with children/young people or vulnerable adults, although not always currently involved in such work in the parish. They should not be the incumbent or his or her partner.*'

8. The role of the PSO is outlined in section 3 of Roles 2017.
9. Some parishes do not have their own website. In this situation, the parish may want to offer some information on the A Church Near You website.
10. Regular reporting means a minimum of twice a year to the PCC.
11. Church Representation Rules 9(2A).
12. This does not include hiring by private individuals for private events, e.g. a child's birthday party.
13. This relates to a clergy vacancy in a benefice and is known as an interregnum.

2. What can a Parish Expect from the Diocese?
14. Please note that the group is called a number of different names in dioceses, e.g. the Diocesan Safeguarding Group, Diocesan Safeguarding Management Group and the Diocesan Safeguarding Advisory Panel.
15. For further information, please see the government's advice on whistleblowing or the safeguarding section of your diocesan website.

3. Abuse and Neglect of Children
16. Further information is available in the Types of Abuse Fact Sheet ❶.
17. This is because impairment caused by seeing or hearing the ill treatment of another (e.g. witnessing domestic violence or abuse) is included in the definition of 'harm' in the Children Act 1989. For more information, see the Responding Well to Domestic Abuse Policy and Practice Guidance ❶.
18. The Protection of Children Act 1978, Section 1.

4. Abuse and Neglect of Adults
19. Further information is available on the Type of Abuse Fact Sheet ❶.
20. Further information is available from the Carers Trust.
21. The Care Quality Commission (CQC). Also note that The Parliamentary and Health Ombudsman (PHSO) deals with complaints that relate to the NHS, including GP services.
22. The Local Government and Social Care Ombudsman.
23. The Prison and Probation Ombudsman.

24. The Clewer Initiative is currently supporting parishes to recognise and raise awareness of all aspects of modern slavery. For further information, see anti-slavery partnerships at Unseen.

5. Safer Recruitment

25. See the Safer Recruitment Practice Guidance ❶ for further information.
26. This is either an enhanced criminal record check with barring information or an enhanced criminal record check without barring information. See Safer Recruitment Practice Guidance, appendices 7 and 8 for further information.
27. For further details about the recruitment of overseas applicants see the Safer Recruitment Practice Guidance.
28. This may be six months for paid roles, depending on the contract, and shorter for unpaid roles.
29. See section 11.

6. Safeguarding Training

30. See the Safeguarding Training and Development Practice Guidance ❶ for further guidance.
31. Please note that this is not an exhaustive list but aims to cover the most common roles in a parish.

7. Responding Promptly to Every Safeguarding Concern or Allegation

32. A 'church officer' is anyone appointed/elected by or on behalf of the Church to a post or role, whether they are ordained or lay, paid or unpaid, for example a priest, church warden, bell-ringer, organist or youth activity leader.
33. Please see the House of Bishops' Responding to, Assessing and Managing Safeguarding Concerns or Allegations Against Church Officers Practice Guidance 2017 for further information.
34. Please note that this includes a concern about a church officer's behaviour that is not in line with safer working practices as outlined in section 11.

35. The person about whom a safeguarding concern or allegation has been made. Sometimes called the 'subject of concerns or allegations' or 'alleged perpetrator'.
36. This would normally be a Parish Safeguarding Officer, incumbent, archdeacon and DSA. It may also be an activity leader if the concern arose within an activity.
37. This means the Local Authority and/or the police.
38. If concerns arise outside of normal office hours, contact the diocesan out-of-hours service.
39. Please note that in some areas this is called the Multi Agency Safeguarding Hub (MASH). In some areas this will be for children only; in other areas it will be for both children and adults.
40. Please note that the LADO should be the first point of contact. They will then inform the police, as required.
41. The person about whom a safeguarding concern or allegation has been made. Sometimes called the 'subject of concerns or allegations' or 'alleged perpetrator'.
42. This means the Local Authority and/or the police.
43. This means abuse disclosed by an adult which happened to them in the past, either as a child or as a younger adult; and abuse disclosed by a child which happened to them in the past as a younger child.
44. Please note that any safeguarding concern or allegation made against a church officer who has died must also be reported to the DSA.
45. For further information please see House of Bishops' Responding Well to Domestic Abuse Practice Guidance 2017.
46. More information for parishes about the new data protection regime can be found at www.parishresources.org.uk/gdpr
47. There are also provisions that allow the sharing of personal data without consent for the prevention or detection of unlawful acts or to protect members of the public from dishonesty, malpractice or seriously improper conduct. However, you should always seek legal advice before relying on these provisions.

48. Information Sharing – Advice is for practitioners providing safeguarding services to children, young people, parents and carers (July 2018).

8. Caring Pastorally for Victims/Survivors of Abuse and Affected Others

49. Please see Forgiveness and Reconciliation in the Aftermath of Abuse for further information.
50. See section 1.4 of Responding to, Assessing and Managing Safeguarding Concerns or Allegations Against Church Officers Practice Guidance 2017.
51. Please see House of Bishops' Responding Well to Those Who Have Been Sexually Abused Practice Guidance 2011 for further information.

9. Caring Pastorally for Church Officers who are the Subject of Concerns or Allegations of Abuse and Affected Others

52. The term 'respondent' refers to the person about whom a safeguarding concern or allegation has been made. Sometimes called the 'subject of concerns or allegations' or 'alleged perpetrator'. This should not be confused with the term 'respondent' that is used under the CDM to describe the person who is the subject of a complaint.
53. See section 1.5 of Responding to, Assessing and Managing Safeguarding Concerns or Allegations Against Church Officers Practice Guidance 2017.

10. Responding to Those who May Present a Known Risk to Children, Young People or Vulnerable Adults within a Christian Congregation

54. Please see section 7 of the House of Bishops' Responding to, Assessing and Managing Safeguarding Concerns or Allegations Against Church Officers Practice Guidance 2017 for further information.
55. Powers of arrest should not be exercised by anyone who does not have the knowledge of the legal requirements of arrest because if a person were to be manhandled in circumstances which went beyond the arrest powers, the person carrying out the arrest (and perhaps the body/organisation which appointed that person) could be sued for assault and/or false imprisonment for any period of detention.

56. An individual has the right to attend acts of worship at the church of the parish within which they reside.

11. A Safe Environment and Activities

57. Please see the Safer Environment and Activities Practice Guidance for further information. This will be available shortly.
58. Please see the Model Code of Safer Working Practice in Safer Environment and Activities Practice Guidance.
59. These ratios are based on NSPCC guidance.
60. The information in these forms should be reviewed annually or as and when it changes i.e. if a child is diagnosed with a medical condition/allergy etc. It will normally be completed by a parent.
61. This means an activity that takes place away from church premises.

Appendix – Information on Vulnerable Adults

62. Section 6 of the Safeguarding and Clergy Discipline Measure 2016.

Acknowledgments

Thanks are owed to Garry Johnson, the previous DSA of Peterborough Diocese, and the Dioceses of Canterbury, Southwark, Peterborough and Newcastle and their parishes for their contribution to the preparation of this practice guidance. Additional thanks go to the other DSAs, too many to name, who have offered their expertise to this guidance, and to the Dioceses of Peterborough, Chelmsford, Oxford, Southwark and Canterbury for the use of some of their materials.